portfolio collection **Piper Shepard**

Author: William Easton
Poetry: H.L. Hix
Editor: Matthew Koumis
Graphic Design: Rachael Dadd & MK
Reprographics: Ermanno Beverari
Printed in Italy by Grafiche AZ

© Telos Art Publishing 2003

Telos Art Publishing
PO Box 125, Winchester
SO23 7UJ England
T: +44 (0) 1962 864546
F: +44 (0) 1962 864727
E: editorial@telos.net
E: sales@telos.net
W: www.telos.net

ISBN 1 902015 81 9 (softback)
ISBN 1 902015 82 7 (hardback)

A CIP catalogue record for this book is
available from The British Library

Notes
All dimensions are shown in metric and
imperial, height x width x depth.

Photo Credits
Dan Meyers, Michael Spillers, Derek
Porter, Anne Lindberg, E.G. Schempf

Artist's Acknowledgments
I thank Laura Burns, Angela Anderson
Adams, and William Easton for such
beautifully accomplished writing. And,
thank you to H.L. Hix for poetry that
provided me new possibilities.

My gratitude to those who have helped in
the studio, in particular, Mellissa Rudder,
Adam Fowler, Jill Gordon, Michele Basta,
Anthea Zeltzman, Caitlin Walsh, and Marie
Gardeski. I am indebted to Beverly Ahern,
Jann Rosen-Queralt, and Jyung Mee Park
for their feedback. Many thanks to my
supportive colleagues and friends at
Maryland Institute College of Art. And,
thank you to my family for their continuous
caring and support.

Publisher's Acknowledgments
Thanks to Erin Prues, Kristina Detwiller,
Simone and Freya.

Cover Illustrations:
front:
Chambers (detail)
2002
handcut cloth, ink, steel

back:
Lattice (detail)
2001
handcut cloth, graphite, steel armature

illustration on page 1 & 48:
Chambers (detail)
2002
handcut cloth, ink, steel

portfolio collection
Piper Shepard

TELOS

Contents

Survey: Terrain and Topographies (detail)
Piper Shepard and Anne Lindberg
1994
screen printed cloth,
wood structure, carved wood
150 x 192 x 108in
(390 x 499 x 281cm)

Foreword

There is something extraordinary about Piper Shepard's work. At first glance, the gossamer quality of her wall-sized textile sculptures suggest sacred space. Upon closer inspection, the beauty of their surfaces reveal a mesmerizing variety of techniques employed. Shepard patiently brings her sizeable works into being through the repetitive processes of sewing, cutting, printing, etching and dyeing. Saturating the cloth with her labor, she gradually tests its resilience, a process akin to the way feelings penetrate our bodies and the endurance of pain or the experience of joy trys our souls.

Shepard's unflagging commitment to craft is remarkable. Her hand has touched literally every thread of every work. A reverence for the handmade, and desire that her work not be taken for granted is revealed in the intentional gesture of leaving a needle and thread hanging from the work or small section unfinished.

Taken as a whole, these labor-rich, vast surfaces of patterned cloth read as homage to the cumulative industry of humankind.

The rectilinear supports that Shepard uses - from two by four framing to a single beam over which a textile medium is draped - suggest architecture while also referring to the rigors of Modernist geometric abstraction in painting and sculpture. The boundless organic patterns of her surfaces delimited by the straight edge of their supports or the edge of the fabric itself form a measured balance. More recently, like a garden left to naturalize over time, the textile skins of Shepard's sculptures appear to reject the geometry of their physical supports, outgrowing them and slipping off their frame. Her move towards greater transparency and lighter color, along with a rejection of the frame, lend an ethereal quality to her recent work.

In the opposition between the hard and soft aspects of human existence Lao-tzu in the Tao Te Ching has said, "The hard and stiff will be broken, The soft and supple will prevail." Shepard's surrender to softness is an exquisite turn of events, allowing the essential organic quality of her work to prevail, accenting the radiant beauty of the textile surface that is her hallmark.

Angela Anderson Adams
Director of Community and Public Art
Cultural Affairs Division
Arlington County, VA, USA

Quiet Studies: unravelling
1993
screen printing and mixed media
on canvas and wood
68 x 42in (177 x 109cm)

Essay   by William Easton

Yardage for Chambers
2002
handcut cloth, ink, steel
180 x 153 x 20in (468 x 398 x 52cm)

Slowly swiftly

With the pile of used X-ACTO blades mounting in a bowl like discarded pistachio shells Piper Shepard is cutting cloth. The number eleven in her hand moves with the grace of experience. Like a figure skater she describes elegant arabesques on a roll of white canvas. She is following the guide of a drawn pattern that seems to be somewhere between William Morris and Iznik. Another pile grows of the discarded shards and splinters of material that have been removed from the roll of cloth. Shepard has been working on this one for about two months. The scroll unwinds gradually, slowly, repeat, slowly. The blade cuts into the cloth adeptly, swiftly, repeat, swiftly.

Repetition nurtures

Children learn to speak through constant repetition, 'plane, plane, plane', 'dog, dog, dog', 'president, president, president'. Parents who speak two languages to their children listen as the child makes seamless joins in the fabric of speech. Formal education, the imposed order of rules and exceptions invites mistakes. The child who a year earlier declined the plural form perfectly now has problems with sheep and sheeps and fish and fish. The querulous regulation of syntax and grammar work against the mnemonics of the nursery. As adults we have the hardest time to learn a new language. Declining the pluperfect of 'amo' or learning irregular German verb endings seems so separate from the act of communicating. Disjointing the body of language from its skeletal structure turns learning into an academic, intellectual feat of mental conjuring.

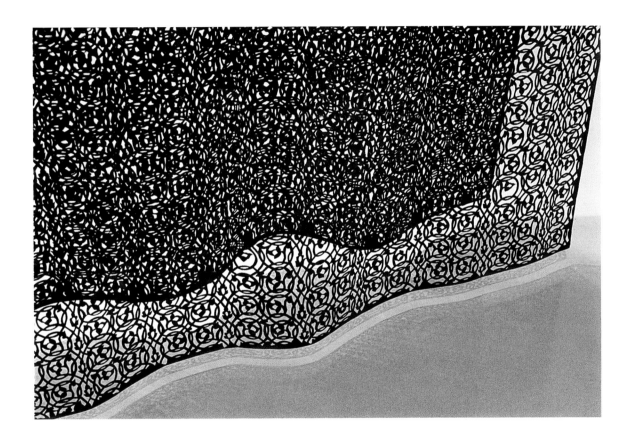

Screen
(detail)
2001
handcut cloth, graphite

There is body knowledge. Constantly repeating, practicing is how we teach the body. It doesn't matter if this is practicing the piano, cutting stone, gutting fish or kicking a football, there comes a moment when the body takes over, can 'make moves' that are known. Shepard's methodology has for many years focused on repeated actions. Her works are all labour intensive, requiring incessant reiteration of a method of manufacture. These have included layer upon layer of screen-printing, drawing, redrawing, frottage, etching, and most recently cutting. She has become incredibly adept at such techniques. The value in learning as a language the physical manipulation of material cannot in a society hooked on book-learnt epistemology claim the supposed dignity of an intellectual pursuit.

Embroidery is a 'humble' craft when compared with say, playing chess, even if the latter seems to be little else but a self-fulfilling exercise. It would however be entirely wrong to suggest that the techniques that Shepard uses are simply a way of getting something done. If we separate the process of making from one of discovery we have prejudiced at the very outset cerebration over corporeality. Like many artists working in contemporary textiles and fiber art such a separation is at best irrelevant and at worst insulting. Shepard has learnt to 'draw' with a knife, but it is not the skill in itself that is any way the aim. In works that take such a long time her process of discovery is multiple, it is directed both at the self and through it. It is marked by moments of seeing, feeling, and at last knowing.

Perhaps even before birth but certainly immediately afterwards the possibilities of language become limited. Even before we can speak we have adopted the biases of our mother tongues. This is a process of focusing, we loose the innate ability to make any of the millions of noises that we humans use to communicate to each other and turn our ears to those of our own 'native' languages. We surrender the possibility of sound for the instrumentality of the spoken. For the child, the choice of language is not their own, but as adults we have that choice. As an artist Shepard has chosen to extend the limits of the given vocabulary to train the reluctant tongue.

Lattice (detail)
2001
handcut cloth, graphite, steel armature

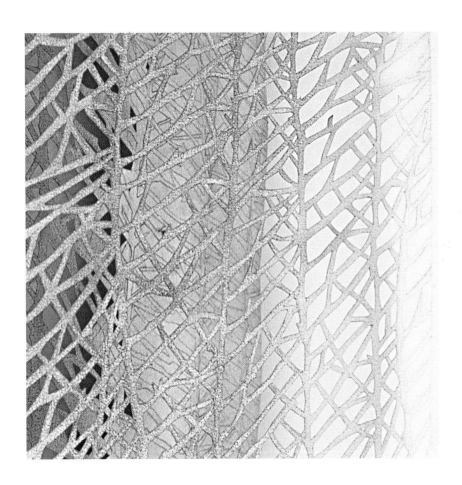

Framing

Piper Shepard's work draws an intriguing trajectory. From her earliest undergraduate false starts to her highly successful work of the last ten years she has retained a formally exact language, an occasionally rigid adherence to structure and a disciplined handling of material process. There is virtually no colour in her work, an austere palate of greys and browns that seem more the result of function than of visual play. Surfaces are treated with graphite, salt, ink and black sand or left bare and raw. A modernist sensibility coupled with a contemporary investigation of material origin, structural complexity and process.

For many, perhaps most contemporary textile artists the point of departure is weaving. For centuries artists have celebrated and challenged the perpendicular constraint of the loom, pushing towards the digital and structured or towards openness and three-dimensionality.

The origins of textiles are shelter and clothing. Anni Albers argued that architecture and textiles had historically been viewed as antithetic, the permanent and grounded against the malleable and movable. By calling a piece of cloth 'a pliable plane' Albers questioned this assertion and invited a host of new inquiry.

For many artists, Shepard included, Albers' questions are still current. In her legacy, weaving escapes the studio and becomes the grid system of the city, the lines of a map, the framework of a house. Cloth becomes, skin, roof, wall, obstacle, divider and pattern. Shepard's work of the nineties repeatedly returned to questions of structure. Rigid armatures, stiff rectilinear forms, support supple bolts of treated cloth that in turn became walls, openings and enclosures. In this work scale shifts, the world opens up as birds eye view and shrinks down to the removal of single threads of cloth.

Enclose
1997
screen printed cloth, devoré,
wood, duratrans, steel
96 x 96 x 4in (250 x 250 x 11cm)

Shepard employed the devoré technique in much of this work that etches into cloth. On the microscopic level the thinness of cloth becomes breadth. But it would be wrong to think that Shepard's fascination in these works is primarily about this scale shift. There is nothing alchemical here, where alchemy circles the idea that what is above is also reflected below, what is seen at a large scale is mirrored at the small. Shepard is not concerned with magic nor is her impulse either allegorical or poetic. In these works structure is not a metaphor or metonymy, it stands in for nothing other than itself and in this respect the work is very American. In much of American arts and letters particularly in the applied arts, the high ascetic of European formalist thinking and the pipedreams of eidetic fantasy are rejected as being too stringent on one hand and too romantic on the other. This is replaced with or converted if not to utility then facility.

In Shepard's works cloth can be worked at the level of its manufacture and as a planar material, not in opposition, but as the corollary of process. Within textile arts technical innovation and developing methods of manufacture become a renewable resource that adds repeatedly to the possibilities of form. In this respect Shepard's work emerges with the acknowledged impetus of a history of minimalism and post-minimalism. Here again this ties her work with the way that rigid European formalist and constructivist tendencies became refocused in American art and redirected primarily on process. The works therefore move from wholly abstract notions of formal relational composition and towards a way of making. Shepard's own art therefore is clearly part of an American tradition of fine art textiles and like the best of that tradition it is constantly innovative but retains the discipline and focus of its foundation. What is always added is the maker.

Unrolling

It is revealing, if not surprising, how the concept of ornament has within a western tradition of aesthetics moved from having a socially critical and ceremonial importance to being understood as useless. Not simply without function but futile, redundant, worthless. One can easily preface the word ornamental with such pejoratives as 'just' 'only' and 'merely', it seems almost out of the question to add such descriptions as 'radical' 'ground breaking' or 'avant-garde'. Even within classical music where ornamentation is the cornerstone of musical complexity and later of virtuosity it is seen as distinctly un-modern. In the middle of the fourteenth-century the Vatican decreed the abolition of ornamental decoration in music completely without success. Humankind seems unable to sing, dance or build without embellishment.

Studio 2002

Shepard's most recent work is intentionally and unabashedly ornamental representing a dramatic departure for the artist. But this is ornament on a grand scale, turning it from decorative detail to edifice. Like many of her recent pieces the new works tentatively called *'Chambers'* are room sized. They are not quite architecture more vernacular, human. Long rolls of cloth perforated by pattern that form a series of hangings that both define and enclose space but also form grilled screens to view through. This is radical ornament.

Whilst this work retains Shepard's strict methodological approach the patterns carry the floral whimsy of an Arts and Crafts design, a meeting of filigree, curlicue and cloister. They echo the extraordinary compositions of the American born Mexican composer Conlon Nancarrow. Abjuring traditional musical notation Nancarrow punched holes in player piano rolls to create music often beyond any human capacity to play, complex polyphonic harmonies with hints of ragtime, jazz and Dixieland. Like Nancarrow's, Shepard's recent works are both very human, haptic but also seem impossible and indefinable.

Chambers
(detail)
2002
handcut cloth, ink, steel

Interlude

All artists are collaborative but some artists
are more collaborative than others. Given
the nature of her work Piper Shepard most often
works alone. She has however joined forces most
notably and successfully with fellow fiber artist
Anne Lindberg. She has also on
two occasions worked with poet H.L. Hix.
There is an erudite and brutal grace to Hix's
writing that suits her work well, an exacting
and sometimes merciless beauty. The following
are three of Hix's poems that require no more
introduction than that they are direct responses to
the uncompromising rigour of Shepard's own
practice...

page 22:
Area Distance
1996
screen printed cloth, devoré,
wood, b&w photos
120 x 120 x 180in
(312 x 312 x 468cm)

right:
Survey: Terrain and Topographies
(1994)
Piper Shepard & Anne Lindberg
screen printed cloth, wood structure,
carved wood floor
150 x 192 x 108in (390 x 499 x 281cm)

When Thales learned to measure in his head

the surface of earth became a ledger.

The annual Nile flood that gave us mud

gave us maps, calendars imposed on space,

the tablature of number's song. If light

does not seep through a surface, water will.

Burned skin rises, buried bones find the sea.

Pass through one portal into another.

Drive the square-mile county roads in Kansas.

Count the soft woven squares that conceal us. [2]

by H.L.Hix

Trapped in the meshes of this neural net,

this translucent tissue, so many small

evanescences: voices, butterflies,

bells, assuming shape, a body the gauze

knows by heart. And recites, neck to navel,

nipple to knee. Light shone through thought shows bells

and butterflies clinging, their bright talc wings

sand mandalas tapped out by bent buddhists,

flour-fine voices of past lovers cooing

like doves huddled on a wire in the rain. [3]

by H.L.Hix

Caught in the Meshes
(detail)
1998
screen printed cloth,
devoré, sand, wood

Beneath
(detail, see also p46)
1998
handcut cloth, graphite, steel, b&w photos
94 x 60 x 10in (245 x 156 x 26cm)

Behind your kneecaps. In your left femur.

Radiating through your pelvis, lodging

between lumbar vertebrae. In your teeth.

You can feel grief even there, in your teeth.

It scalds your tongue and throat like hot coffee.

It spreads through you, confident as cancer.

Nothing is so delicious. Nothing feels

more like a bird trapped inside your body,

crashing into walls and windows over

and over while the cruel light pours in. [4]

by H.L.Hix

Screen
(detail)
2001
handcut cloth, graphite

Hooks and pegs

Critics and historians like hooks, convenient pegs from which to thread chronologies, dates, events, influences, and moments of catharsis that help to plot a narrative. In looking at an artist's work over a number of years however, such a way of thinking is both alluring and insufficient. They tend to confuse artist, work and process. Time becomes fluid, an important event here becomes magnified later, a two-year labour becomes condensed to a detail. In looking at Piper Shepard, her art and her way of working one is confronted by the necessary contradictions of such history. Abroad and home are not categories for analysis but echoes of the play between a body of work and an artist.

Chambers
2002
handcut cloth, ink, steel
108 x 4 x 47in (281 x 123 x 123cm)

Abroad

Shepard has travelled widely, through central and southern Europe, Scandinavia, Turkey, India and across North America. She has compiled a lexicon of experiences. What is most telling is the lack of hierarchical privilege that she affords them. A collection of nineteenth century patterning from The Victoria and Albert Museum in London, a visit to a mosque in India, an afternoon spent in a rug store in Anatolia or an exhibition of contemporary Swedish textile arts can equally play a possible role in her own visual language. As such they first must resonate within her own practice, her own way of thinking. They cannot be borrowed or adopted, but as much as possible must be internalised; otherwise they risk being little else than a collection of tourist snapshots.

Shepard transforms and works through the images of her journeys. They are not exotic quotes, trophies, or souvenirs nor are they treated as holy and untouchable, but as material. Whilst lifting something out of context always runs the risk of misappropriation Shepard's attitude seems simultaneously respectful and also genuinely personal. The treatment of photographs in her work follows a similar path. It is clinical, not indulgent and certainly not romantic. Photographs are stripped of decadence and the resultant images are clean and unadorned. There is no claim of objectivity. They resemble rather than mimic scientific illustration and are both motivated and starkly beautiful.

The following is a list of Shepard's own making,
A list of photographic images that have appeared in
her work shaped like a wing that form a point like a scalpel.

A mosaic of glass and mirror from the Amber Fort in Jaipur
Remnants of a building torn down in Chicago
A carved marble relief from the Taj Mahal
A horizon line where sky and water meet
A detail of a peeling paint
An aerial view of water
A map

right:
Amber Fort
Jaipur, India

left:
Wall Fragment II (detail)
1995
screen printed cloth,
devoré, wood, stacked paper

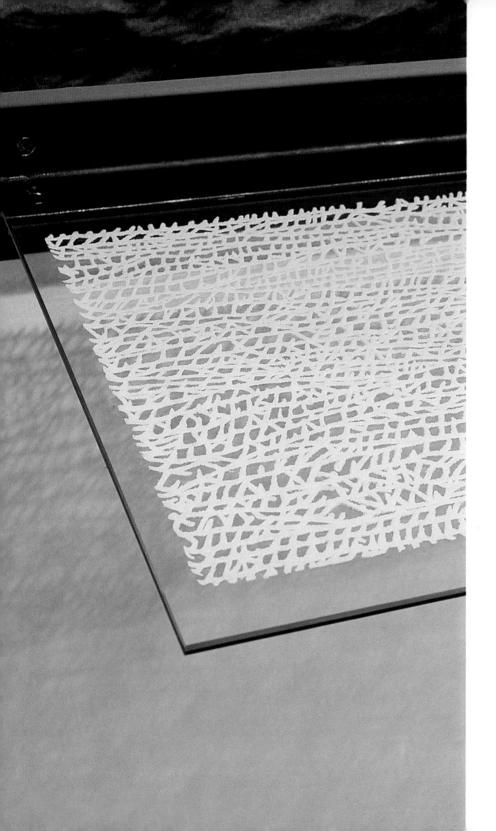

Mantles
2000
handcut cloth, salt, glass,
steel, b&w photographs
94 x 14 x 14in
(245 x 37 x 37cm)

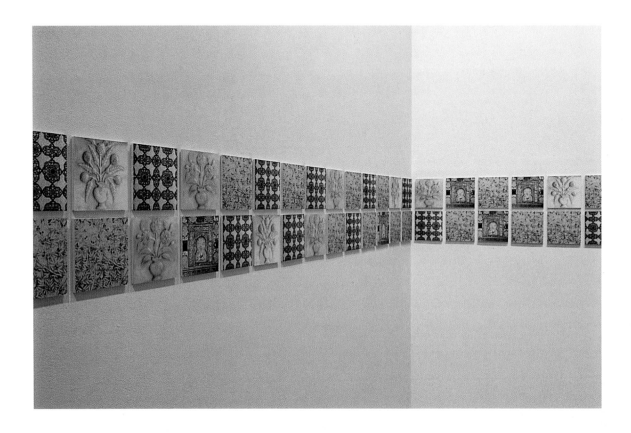

this page:

Tiles 2001

iris prints on wood

4 x 4in (11 x 11cm)

opposite:

White Wall and Screen

2001

handcut cloth, graphite, steel armature

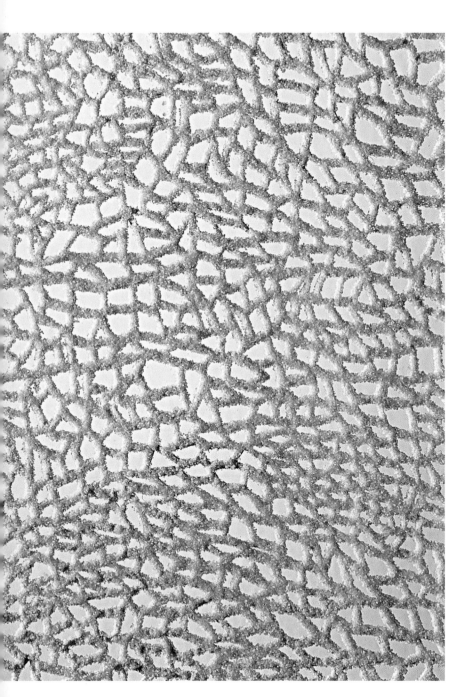

Home

Turkish kilims, paintings by numbers, shell-boxes, jadeite, Bakelite, cloth, fragments of wall-paper; Shepard's home is a collection of collections. In stark contrast to her own work colour abounds. Shepard is not however a true collector, there is none of the minutia of taxonomy. Objects seem like samples, a visual sketchbook of ideas. Having written the last sentences I am surprised at my own rudeness. One might question this inclusion of an artist's private world within a history as being unnecessarily invasive. One can as equally find here, however, the complexity of difference that underscores the maker, the made and the way of making.

Scrollwork

Contemporary fiber art is perhaps no less voguish than any other area of art practice but it does have the advantage of being so diverse as to avoid the more obvious pitfalls of trend. Shepard, like others, has found a secure, supported and self-assured place to work from within the field. She has over a number of years developed works at a pace set by the laborious nature of their manufacture. She looks across a table at me and says three years for the current work. And I am thinking that's longer than it takes for a couple of novels, feature films or a concerto or two.

The time it takes however, is not some marathon dance, a test of endurance, but simply the time it takes. This is integrity. It is possible to speed up a process, cut corners or reduce scale, but what would be lost. There are moments when hearing what was involved in making a piece one wonders if there isn't some easier way. Shepard's reply is revealing, this is the most effective way to do it. It is a rejection of the frenetic pace of living. It is a process of focussing. It is necessary. The pile of blades continues to mount.

William Easton
Stockholm 2002-10-06

Footnotes to the Essay:

1. *Devoré* is a commercial process by
which the application of a chemical
compound removes plant fibres such as
cotton, linen, rayon, ramie, and hemp but
leaves both protein fibres such as silk,
wool as well as synthetics.

2. The poem is a direct response to work in
the exhibition '4 Tangents', El Dorado Inc,
Kansas City, Missouri 1996.
It is quoted with the author's permission from:
Hix, H.L. *Rational Numbers* (Kirksville, MO:
Truman State University Press, 2000).

3, 4. These poems are a contribution to the
collaborative exhibition 'En Response,' The
Writer's Place, Kansas City, Missouri 1999.
They are quoted with the author's permission
from *Rational Numbers* (Kirksville, MO:
Truman State University Press, 2000).

Enclose

1997

screen printed cloth, devoré, wood,

duratrans, steel

4 walls, 96 x 96 x 4in (250 x 250 x 11cm)

Biography

Born	1962, Willimantic, Connecticut

Education and Awards

1985	Philadelphia College of Art, Philadelphia, Pennsylvania, Bachelor of Fine Arts in Fiber
1988	Cranbrook Academy of Art, Bloomfield Hills, Michigan, Master of Fine Arts in Fiber
1997	Individual Artist Award, Maryland State Arts Council
1997	Board of Trustees Award for Excellence in Teaching, Maryland Institute, College of Art
2003	Individual Artist Award, Maryland State Arts Council

Teaching

1994-present	Maryland Institute College of Art, Baltimore, MD
1990-94	Kansas City Art Institute, Kansas City, MO
1989-90	North Carolina State University, School of Design, Raleigh, NC

Selected Exhibitions

2003	'Annet Couwenberg and Piper Shepard,' 28th Street Studio, New York, NY
2001	Sabbatical Exhibition, Decker Gallery, Maryland Institute College of Art, Baltimore, MD
2000	'Artscape,' Decker Gallery, Maryland Institute, College of Art, Baltimore, MD
	'Miniatures2000,' Helen Drutt Gallery, Philadelphia, PA (tour Helsinki Finland)
	'Crosscurrents 2000: Handle with Care, Loose Threads in Fiber,'
	The Art Gallery University of Maryland, College Park, MD

Selected Exhibitions continued

1999	'En Response, The Writer's Place,' Kansas City, MO
1998	'The 1998 Biennial,' Delaware Art Museum, Wilmington, DE
1997	'Transformation: Fiber Orientations, New Applications,' Dowd Fine Arts Gallery, State University of New York College at Cortland, NY
	'An Approximate Geography,' Dolphin Gallery, Kansas City, MO
	'What's in the Air,' The Kansas City Artist Coalition, Kansas City, MO
	'Surface Tensions,' The Center of Contemporary Arts, University City, MO
	'Art Sites,96,' The Corcoran Gallery of Art, Washington, DC and The Elipse Gallery, Alington, VA
	'4 Tangents,' El Dorado, inc, Kansas City, MO
	'Cloth Reveries,' The Janet Wallace Fine Arts Centre, Macalester College, St Paul, MN
	'Uncommon Threads,' Penland School of Crafts, Penland, NC
	'4 Years, 35 Artists,' Dolphin Gallery, Kansas City MO
1995	'material poetry,' Katherine E Nash Gallery, University of Minnesota, Minneapolis, MN
	'Printed Work,' Wagman Gallery, University of the Arts, Philadelphia, PA
1994	'Survey, A Collaborative Work,' by Anne Lindberg and Piper Shepard The Textile Art Centre, Chicago, IL
1993	'Artist's Drawings,' Palm Beach Community College, Palm Beach, FL

1992	'Material Inquiry: Work by Recent MFA Graduates in Fiber,' Janet Wallace Fine Arts Center, Macalester College, St. Paul, MN
1992	'661/7,932 turn, collaborative work by Anne Lindberg and Piper Shepard,' Dolphin Gallery, Kansas City, MO
1990	'The Fiber National,' Access to the Arts, Inc., Adams Art Gallery, Fredonia, NY
	'Designs in Sculptural Fiber,' The Craft Alliance, St. Louis, MO
1989	'The Fiber Art International,' Pittsburgh Center for the Arts, Pittsburgh, PA

Selected Publications & Reviews

2001	*Surface Design Journal*, review of 'Crosscurrents,' by Bonnie Holland, fall
2000	'Obsession,' exhibition brochure
	'Crosscurrents,' exhibition catalogue
1998	*American Craft Magazine*, 'Surface Tension: New Works in Textiles,' by Luanne Rimel, Feb/March
1997	*Fiberarts* Magazine, 'Is There Still a Place for Fiber Art?' Catherine S. Amidon, Nov/Dec
	'Transformation: Fiber Orientations, New Applications,' S.U.N.Y., Cortland, brochure
	'What's in the Air,' by Catherine S. Amidon, Kansas City Artist's Coalition, Kansas City, MO, brochure

Wall Fragment ll
1995
53 x 36 x 5"
screen printed cloth,
devoré, wood, stacked paper

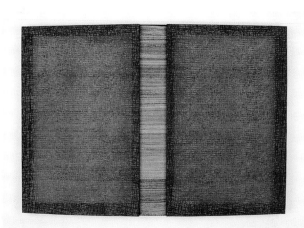

Selected Publications & Reviews (continued)

1997	*Surface Design Journal*, 'Architecture in Textiles,' by Heather Allen, Summer
1996	'4 Tangents,' El Dorado, Inc., brochures
	Cloth Reveries, Macalester College, exhibition catalogue
	'Art Sites 96,' Washington Review, exhibition catalogue
1995	'Material Poetry', University of Minnesota, exhibition catalogue
	Surface Design Journal, exhibition review by Janet Paine, summer
	Fiberarts Magazine, 'Surface Design Breakthrough,' by Gregg Johnson, March/April (reproduction)
1994	*Fiberarts Magazine*, 'Collaboration (and Other Not So Scandalous Plots),' by William Easton, September/October
	'Survey,' Textile Art Centre, brochure
1992	*Surface Design Journal*, exhibition review by Charles Talley, Fall
1991	'Material Inquiry,' Macalester College, exhibition brochure
1990	'Fiber National,' Adams Art Gallery, exhibition brochure
	'The Continuous Process: The Artist as Teacher, The Teacher as Artist,' North Carolina State University, exhibition catalogue

left:

Beneath
1998
handcut cloth, graphite,
steel, b&w photos
94 x 60 x 10in (245 x 156 x 26cm)

right:

Area Distance
1996
120 x 120 x 180"
screen printed cloth,
devoré, wood, b&w photos